About the Author

As a nurse, the author has always been moved to write about life and death, the pains and joys of loving, and most of all, about the wonders of nature. The Philippines, where she grew up, is an archipelagic paradise and Germany, where she currently lives, provides her with scenic ambience; and so she dreams… and writes…

Tell it to the Flowers

Sarah Abegail Villamor

Tell it to the Flowers

Vanguard Press

VANGUARD PAPERBACK

© Copyright 2023
Sarah Abegail Villamor

The right of Sarah Abegail Villamor to be identified as author of this work has been asserted by her in accordance with the Copyright, Designs and Patents Act 1988.

All Rights Reserved

No reproduction, copy or transmission of this publication may be made without written permission.
No paragraph of this publication may be reproduced, copied or transmitted save with the written permission of the publisher, or in accordance with the provisions of the Copyright Act 1956 (as amended).

Any person who commits any unauthorised act in relation to this publication may be liable to criminal prosecution and civil claims for damages.

A CIP catalogue record for this title is available from the British Library.

ISBN 978 1 80016 888 6

*Vanguard Press is an imprint of
Pegasus Elliot Mackenzie Publishers Ltd.*
www.pegasuspublishers.com

First Published in 2023

**Vanguard Press
Sheraton House Castle Park
Cambridge England**

Printed & Bound in Great Britain

Great thanks to my Manito- and Jimenez-Villamor Family (Philippines), Klabuhn Family (Germany), and friends (you know who you are) who inspired me to create this gem.

To Pegasus Publishers, thank you for making this dream of mine come true.

To God. You're the best!

To those who relish dreaming while awake, this precious gem is for you.

What's Inside?

Lotus	13
To the Water Hyacinths	14
Lilies and Hyacinths	15
Rhodora	17
Baby's Breath	18
Rosette	19
Orchard of Immortal Gladness	20
Floral Memories	21
Blossoms	22
The Dance of Romance	23
Growing in Each Other's Heart	24
The Love Trap	26
Unrequited Love	28
A Heart Made of Snowflakes	29
The Heart is a Fragile Thing	30
Speak of Heartaches	32
A Bird's Wish	33
Sofa Syllables	34
Dream Weaver	35

Alluring Beauty	36
Everlasting Youth	37
Ink Spill	38
A Beautiful Garment	39
Sweet Somnolence	40
Lifeline	41
Ethical Excellence	42
Stardust	43
Dusk	44
Living	45
Being Underneath	46
Clash, Flash, and Crash	47
Virgo	48
Flourescence	49
Listen	50
Melancholia	52
The Night's Silhouette	53
Elusive Illusions	54
June Birthstones	55
Dare	56
Being Human	57
Envy	58

Wordless Melody	59
From Far Away	60
Fearless	61
Mathematical Relationship	62

Lotus
Sonnet

Aye, aye, sun of Egypt, my heart is torn!
Lost, I surrender; love can't be reborn.
Skies above, but I never knew you can
Awaken the spirit of any man.

Thou blessed the earth with stars though never fall.
In beauty's death, life is yours to enthrall.
Leaves untouched by water in its own nest,
Thou freed this soil from carcass where sins rest.

Tell me, Lotus, thy secret to vict'ry,
Why in stain thou preserve thy purity?
Give me, thus, the sweetness of thy perfume
That I may taste the prowess you assume.

When in perfection you so beguile me,
I win back love and give that love to thee.

To the Water Hyacinths

Under the old bridge might there be a soul, I wondered
As I went down the slope to join the sleepy water.
Then the moon showed up and moonbeams showered
So I might see the little wonders on the pillow of the river.

On the shimmering blue water, in the night's pale gray,
Floated the evening mistresses, perhaps weary after a day.
Covering the resting watercourse with their wild array,
So do my eyes on their beauty feast as long as I may.

Water hyacinths, in thy purplish cheeks, power and passion
    you keep.
Hopeful is this heart, your leaves of comfort will heal its scars
    so deep.
Bring forth your flame ethereal and stay yonder while I sleep.
So that tonight, may my goodbye be final, in heaven at least
    will I sleep.

Lilies and Hyacinths

water lilies,
the proud,
smile more beautifully than
the flora near the clay
in reality,
the sun pours its glorious rays on them
seldom,
they hide their lovely faces,
the blossoms amidst the silver lake
sway more gracefully in the breeze than
the humble
water hyacinths

---

water hyacinths,
the humble,
sway more gracefully in the breeze than
the blossoms amidst the silver lake,
they hide their lovely faces
seldom,
the sun pours its glorious rays on them

in reality,
the flora near the clay
smile more beautifully than
the proud
water lilies

Rhodora

Deep within a forest's heart,
A lovely flower lies.
Without a leaf, yet full of charm,
And hung with butterflies.

A beauty rare amidst the wild -
That accounts the flower best.
A purplish blossom so dear as a child,
A gift of joy upon the world's request.

Rhodora, a name graced with fairness;
Yet only part of the earth knows
That she preserves not just the slightest touch of greatness,
Indeed, she is the rival of the rose.

Baby's Breath

Early morning buds kiss the dew of dawn
Little white petals dance into garden tones
Velvety rain whispered in a ribbon
Inspires the Earth to offer what it owns
Reeling hazily to the sound of the torrent
Aspirant of love, a Baby's Breath, meek and ardent

Rosette

Rosette in bloom,
    thou have vanquished my heart's gloom.
Oh, thou art a charade,
    a nectar's parade!
Some say how fierce
    those thorns of thine do pierce,
And hail themselves judge
    of thy hues with grudge.
Not merely thy presence
    but thy essence
Can bring a man to kill,
    all for thy will.

Orchard of Immortal Gladness

Love's perennial air's thy perfume.
Orchard of immortal gladness
Revealed its beauty to thine eyes.
It is, I know, as I could guess,
Ethereal blossom at thy price.

Floral Memories

Mem'ries are like flowers.
Some are sweet, others are yet sweeter.
Some quickly wilt, just for a day.
Others long last, from May 'til May.
Many are as lovely as a lover's caress.
Sometimes they sleep
And are awakened by the fires of summer.

Blossoms
Haiku

The flowers of May,
Whether still buds or in bloom,
Bring joy to the day.

The Dance of Romance
Sonnet

Let me dance to the sonata of spring,
Whence the tune of emotions come endless;
To give the warmth of a fire that's burning
And express pain whilst the heart's not painless.

Love's a choice fate forbids not to lovers,
That the dancer's tiptoes forward the claim.
Each step, not by chance, follows the seekers.
The notes on the ledger lines get the blame.

Every time the feet grow limp of dancing,
A pair succeeds, the music goes on still.
The law of romance in heart is lacking.
Succinctly it is for it's ours to fill.

Love's great danger is not to tip and fall,
But to leave the dance floor and lose it all.

Growing in Each Other's Heart

We've shared our dreams when laughter
Was the life of our days.
We've always been together,
Sang our songs in many ways.

Children have we been before,
Have thought love was just a game.
Now we grew a little more,
I wonder how we're still the same.

Songbirds die and apples rot,
On the same tree they both rest.
So the flame we watered not
Will die with us in its crest.

In our palms a promise lies,
That we'll weave more dreams each day.
If one shall dare leave our eyes,
We'll both find it on our way.
Once we taught and once we knew
The lesson this world did have:
Paint the years with colors true,
And see the essence of love.

Like leaves nourished in a seed,
We grow in each other's heart.
At dawn, we're like scattered weeds,
At dusk, we become one part.

The Love Trap

His eyes were cold,
His lips were pale,
    but he learned to paint them red
He put on a white robe,
    tattooed the sunshine into his irises,
He traded his tail with wings
    from an innocent swan
        he just so recently killed.

When he knocked at my door,
    he carried in his arms the moon
        and behind him a basket full of stars.
I wondered what he was hiding behind his turban,
    but I forgot to ask
        when he flashed at me a very beautiful smile

I let him in,
    invited him to sit on my visitor's couch.
But even before he could take a seat,
    he asked what that room was
        with the closed door upstairs,

to which I didn't answer.

I offered him snacks,
    let him choose between coffee or tea,
but he didn't want any of those,
said he brought honey instead.

He then showed me a pendulum,
    swung it in front of my face,
and until now…
I am still running in my dream…

Unrequited Love

The vividness of you as you walk towards me
Sends a thrilling sensation down my spine.
But your footsteps are light, I can barely hear them,
And there's something in the way you walk I can't
    define.

There's only euphoria having you by my side,
And even more when you asked, "Can you be mine?"
The stream of happiness felt so unreal
Because there's something in the way you talk that's so
    divine.

Then I woke up from a long and deep sleep,
And released were the imaginings that pleased my mind.
I hope this love that in my heart I keep
Will be the same love in your heart you'll find.

A Heart Made of Snowflakes

The winds whisper a sad melody
Which penetrates into her lonely soul.
Coldness soon replaces her warmth
While it drains her blood.

Into the shadows creeps the memory of a past
Whose years were tainted with agony.
She flees to the entrance of eternity
To finally see the light and free herself.

Gradually, snowflakes consume her dying heart
And banish the history that was painted on her face.
Forever will she relish every fear and every pain
And despise the pleasures of love.

The Heart is a Fragile Thing

The heart is a glass of water
That easily breaks.
Don't strike it with a hammer,
There will flow a thousand creeks.

The heart is a mirror
That reflects the true you.
Don't cut it with a razor,
You'll break your heart in two.

The heart is a bottle
Containing tasty wine.
Don't hit it with a pebble,
You'll end up with a whine.

The heart is an eyeglass
Through which you clearly see the world.
Without it, don't let a day pass,
You'll regret it when you're old.

The heart is not a carbonic stone,
Whose molecules so tightly cling.
It shatters once it is alone.
It is a fragile thing.

Speak of Heartaches

Clouds of ashen black veil the sunlit eyes
Of the freshly dessicated skies.
Slivers of rain caged in ice
Once fell, now plummet twice.

Rampant waters swallowed underneath
The snowy earth with bloody sheath
Seek orifice distances beneath
White grounds, swathed in death.

Heaven's violent hammers are whence
All catastrophes commence,
Crushing the toughest, hence,
Glaciers are fragile, however dense.

A Bird's Wish

I was once in your hands,
But you let me fly away.
You're one who understands
Always, but not today.

    If you're hungry, eat me then,
    And I'll take my death with pride.
    Who told you I wanted freedom when
    Freedom means to leave your side?

        I beg you to capture me again,
        And consume me if you wish.
        For I'd rather by your hands be slain
        Than die and be another hunter's dish.

Sofa Syllables
Quatern

Do re mi fa so la ti do
In my senses they come and go.
A chord played by my fingertips
Is music from my silent lips.

The bouncing bars of the piano,
Do re mi fa so la ti do
Strike the keys in decrescendo.
Do ti la so fa mi re do

From do to mi, then ti to do
From you to me and me to you
Do re mi fa so la ti do
My heart dances in staccato.

The hammers' impact on the strings
Puts tones to it and then it sings:
I'll wait until you say "I do"
Do re mi fa so la ti do

Dream Weaver
Quatern

She roams the sky and plucks a star
And weaves a magic tapestry.
She lays it on a silver bar
Below the moon, above the sea.

Humming a song into your head,
She roams the sky and plucks a star.
Stardust she sprinkles on your bed
And takes you to some places far.

She keeps fireflies in fairies' jars.
Their golden tails cast light in streams.
She roams the sky and plucks a star
And sings her way inside your dreams.

Her midnight eyes moon-gray in light
Invites the breeze to where you are.
And when you lie and say "goodnight,"
She roams the sky and plucks a star.

Alluring Beauty
Sonnet

To fool a man to love, why waste a wile
When beauty alone can silence his wits?
Thou have dazed most men though repressed a smile
And have cast a spell on them you bewitch.

True, the sun to the earth its radiance shows
And its highness gazed upon for being
Its light does outshine all us flames below
But in fairness thou art more outstanding.

In a look, my eyes can tell I'm impressed
By the inner charm that surfaces still
Even beneath the brilliance of thy vest
That will deceive those hearts you're yet to steal.

When these lines upon you and me agreed,
I declare thine allure can sate one's greed.

Everlasting Youth
Sonnet

Whatever part of thee in youth shall glow,
When comes the time you feared white hairs may grow.
As torches with flames blazing more aglow,
When the sun is down, when the night winds blow.

Thy soul that freshly filters through thine eyes
Of mem'ry arrested and pain all healed.
I ask – shall thou to world still disguise
That novel wisdom to me you've revealed?

Now, in oblivion, thy put the seasons:
The snow of winters, save the summer's fire.
Thy cold heart betrayed itself for reasons
To beseech its warmth by its own desire.

For youth, through golden days, never expires.
A child dead in his tomb no one aspires.

Ink Spill
Acrostic

Inspired by the sages
    Never after ages
        Killed the pen's heart

Slept not this art
    Poets still dare to write
        Indelible sketches in white
            Luminous in black sheet
                Living in blood and sweat

A Beautiful Garment

Clad in flame thy spirit, whence joyousness
Hath, by tint and shade, been an ornament.
Regardless what hue paints thy youthfulness,
In the transparency of its garment,
Shall be displayed without uncertainty.
Thus however thou perfumeth thy soul,
In whiche'er way thou weaveth its tapestry,
Not shalt by any measure change but one;
Extinguished be that fire once love there's none.

Sweet Somnolence

Chaotic, the rendezvous of thoughts
Confusing, speeches a mixture of noise and music,
The tender shrill of the thrilling air
Was nowhere to be heard.
Nonetheless, the Earth is without bound,
Peace sleeps on dreams
Whence resonates every gentle sound,
And bewildering emotions cleared
When in time I rode with nature's fare,
Lulled and pacified – a pleasant frolic,
Tranquil, my world drifted from my thoughts/

Lifeline

Look beyond your years and sigh,
Indeed what a weary life it can be.
End crawls nearer with a sleepy eye,
Zooming out the lifelines of a tree.
Empty past makes some men's future empty.
Love and lust - the latter's a folly.
Death and life, you say it's rather death than pain
To choose when obstacles in front of you are lain.
Remember though that happiness roots from sacrifice.
Obey the winds, adjust your sails, and be wise.
The strong is strong because he endures,
And walks straight to his destination past the lures.

Ethical Excellence
Acrostic

Every learner, in life, is a philosopher
To question what's unknown, what's unseen.
His own mind provides the seeker's answer
In this universe of what is yet and what has been.
Call the judge and he'll look upon what's inside.
A satisfied brain may mean an empty heart.
Like a keen dagger for one's precious pride
Expertly sharpened for a sinful art.
Cast your ken of the pheromone of men
Equivocal to an extent that language may seem.
Lay your hands on the table bare and open.
Light up a generous flame once your paths are dim.
Ethos is a seed you sowed to reap.
No one plants for a fruit not aspired.
Coming from the core with its roots embedded deep,
Emanates from it the excellence you desired.

Stardust

When life becomes tiring,
Just look up into the heavens and see
The stardust that keeps on falling.
They are the dreams you've made
On your blissfully woven days.

Dusk

The dusk the flowers all are waiting for
Will soon come and fold their charms to rest.
After a dream, they'll dream once more
To meet their everlasting sleep upon heaven's behest.

Living

Living is wandering in a vast desert.
As you walk, you keep on chasing hopes.
The fine sands where you tread are little joys.
Possibilities are not always seen -
At times you'll find an oasis.
Often will sandstorms catch you in their breast.
But whatever happens,
In the desert one thing is certain;
Always will you leave traces of footsteps,
Marks that will let others know
That you have walked there once.

Being Underneath

The rocks that lie below the water cascades
Never wait in vain but instead rejoice,
For unto them fall the glory of the mountains.

Clash, Flash, and Crash

Ice and fire
Meet in the firmament.
Light then sound follow ire,
Stirring Earth's temperament.

Virgo

Astral allure of tresses fair
Noble veil with Virgo flair
Nestles stars whose perfection share
Innate radiance beyond compare
Elegance as constant as air

Meteors across the sky traverse
A shower born but to rehearse
Rain must to thee their textured tears
So might thou find thine oldest verse
Heavenly strung with lines transverse
Awakened from its slumber years

A stentorian thunder of ire
Bludgeoning sound from ice and fire
Abandons liquors of desire
Yet thou art still filled, not to expire
And having reached thou dost aspire
Nothing but peace thou shalt require

Flourescence

Vows of summertime die on the flowers
Array of sunbeams to moonrise lowers
Lavender mists pierce the clouds of saffron and orange
Etched in the blackness, the hues to rearrange
Now even in midnight, light is of essence
Zealous crafter of diamonds in graphite's non-existence
Unleash the spirit cloaked in stone-rigid cells
Echoes of frolic and mirth magnetize all else
Let live and lived while life is all jocund
A limitless joy though unknown is what's beyond

Listen

The raindrops make a distinct sound as they touch a surface.
So when it rains and when it doesn't, everybody need not guess.
But who would know if the patter came from a mound or a pit?
I say, it's the one who listens well who can answer it.

Listening is a skill the sky had long perfected.
When the earth is dry and thirsty, the generous rain pours.
This you might wonder, why of such a voiceless soil, the need the sky had captured.
My friend, you must know and learn how the sky had listened for hours.

So when the creator of the sky and the rain speaks in a voice you cannot hear,
Try to close your eyes, as well as your ears.
Use the ear of your heart instead and listen reverently.

And there, louder than your heartbeat, you'll hear His voice very clearly.

Melancholia

I sit here in this empty room.
The statues watch me with eyes of gloom.
The scattered chairs, the open door,
The silent cold wind sweeping by the floor
Display the lifeless churchroom more
Lonesome than the me I was before.

The Night's Silhouette

The darkness that feeds the night
Is interrupted by a single light.
I looked at the light-flooded pavement and realized
That my silhouette is black amidst the white.
Without the luminosity perhaps I wouldn't see
That the dark part of the night is actually me.

Elusive Illusions

Just what lingering emotions
Engraved in her cemented heart
Shalt she but keep once come a time
Serve well thee mustn't for her dime?
Oblivion is not for such art
Not, for elusive illusions
Await even in thy rope's end…

June Birthstones

Alexandrite…
    with colors bright,
    you never failed
    to make her blithe

        Pearl…
            dancing with a twirl,
            you make her heart
            jump and whirl

                Moonstone…
                      as lovely as the dawn
                      but loveliest when
                      the moon had shone

Dare

The spirits, they took away your light.
Hold your own rope.
Jump blindly into the darkness of the night.
Don't let them eat your soul.
They are ghouls.
They aren't yours.

Kill your own demons.
I know you're struggling…
But hold on tight to that hope.

No, that's not the sun.
That's not the moon.
Nevertheless, it's a flicker of light.
Dare to follow it.

I don't know where you are going to.
I don't know what you're going through
Inside…
But follow your will -
The mind of your feet…
The salt of your soul…

Being Human

It's hard to train the mind
To be in the present moment
All the time.

Sometimes,
We tend to drift into a trance,
Where we think about
Our past mistakes.

It's totally okay.

I hope
We can forgive ourselves
For being such…
For being human.

Envy

There's something tastier than meat.
Your soft delicious brain I wanna eat
To get the itch out of my tiny head
And keep my fingers from scratching it dead.

Wordless Melody

Called by a voice beyond that saffron-glowing cirrus
Laid thy heart for that light behind the nimbus
All for love, else only for thee
Reminding me, joy is ever for free
Enthralled, even to pay I will my pride
No questions more, no broken thoughts, my mind need
    not decide
Captive always will I be of thy strummed chord
Endlessly spilling music without a word

From Far Away

The stars reflect how dear you are
How close you seem, though you are far
You're like the sky that shelters me
Raining down joy where you may be
On your cozy clouds I'd love to ride
Not ever to get off, I will decide
Even my deepest secrets to you I'll confide

Fearless

I wouldn't fear death
If it were mine.
My beloved is dead.
But I don't fear death still
Because it happened already.
There's nothing to fear now.
I haven't wished for death either
But
Today…
I wish it were mine.

Mathematical Relationship

Enclosed in a numerical infinity
Our student life is but a lone possibility
We're used to break; we're prone to change
Yet we always stay within our range

All by ourselves, we are constantly
Seeking glimpses of affinity
To describe what mere words cannot say
Through an equation beyond valuable display

We might have traversed all crooked lines
And have averted from the vertex oftentimes
But surely right after every equal sign
We bridge our ways to a single line

Some prime figures we never were
We share our sides, we complement, we extend our care
Sometimes we find our paths divide
But at the end, what matters most:
Together, our answers multiplied…

www.ingramcontent.com/pod-product-compliance
Lightning Source LLC
LaVergne TN
LVHW091934070526
838200LV00068B/1129